Winson Green
My World

by
Gary Smith

Winson Green
My World

by

Gary Smith

with
Foreword by

Dr. Carl Chinn

BREWIN BOOKS

First published October 1997
by Brewin Books, Doric House, Church Street,
Studley, Warwickshire.
Reprinted January 1998
Reprinted May 2001

ISBN 1 85858 108 7

British Library Cataloguing-in-Publication Data.
A catalogue record for this book is available from the British Library.

Typeset in Clearface and
made and printed in Great Britain
by SupaPrint (Redditch) Limited,
Redditch, Worcestershire

FOREWORD

Carl Chinn

They sing about the palm trees swaying down Summer Lane and about the gas works of Saltley. Poems are written about the courtyards of Ladywood and the monkey run of the Coventry Road in Small Heath. Stories are told about the potent smells of Aston and the tantalising aromas of Bournville. And books have been written about life in so many parts of Old Brum - from Lozells in the north to Sparkbrook in the south, from Hockley in the west to Nechells in the east. Yet there's one major working-class neighbourhood that seems to be forgotten in the tales of the old end - Winson Green. Perhaps it's because it's right on the edge of Brum, squeezed tight against the borders with Smethwick. Perhaps it's because no arterial road goes through the district, even though its bounded by the Dudley Road. Or perhaps it's because it was the site of three disliked Victorian institutions - the prison, the asylum and most of all the workhouse.

Yet just like Brummies elsewhere, the folk of Winson Green have made their mark on our city. They've grafted and they've collared, they've shopped and they've mooched, they've canted and they've yapped and they've bonded together to make villages and neighbourhoods. Their lives should not be forgotten. Now they won't be. Winson Green has its own storyteller. Gary Smith has brought to life its streets and entries. He's brought before us its shops and buildings. But most of all he's drawn into view the families and characters of Winson Green - his end.

v

CONTENTS

INTRODUCTION

My late Dad was in Dudley Road Hospital having some tests, and Mom and I on one of our visits were made aware of a new arrival on the ward. Our Dad asked us if we recognised him? Straight away we did, it was our old chemist Mr. Powell. We went up to him and made ourselves known. After the usual chit-chat, Mom went back to Dad, but I stayed awhile to talk to him. He then told me the reasons for coming to Birmingham in the first place. In his lovely soft Welsh accent he told me that, as positions as a chemist were hard to come by in the 30's in Wales, he had applied for a position as manager of a chemist's in Birmingham. It was to be for Bannister and Thatchers. It was on the corner of Lodge Road and Handsworth New Road, Winson Green. His wife didn't come up at that time as she was unsure about coming to a big brash city like Brum. He then told me what he had told his wife many, many years before. All large towns and cities were nothing but little villages joined together, each with their own communities and characters, each with their own churches, schools and shops. Folks would be born in the area, attend the local schools go to churches in the district, get married and probably live just around the corner from their parents, people didn't need to move away as they felt safe on their own patch. It must have done the trick as his wife came up and never went back. As he said, you would have felt comfortable as you would know most people in your own area and they would have known you, or your family. Mr. Powell would then have been in his late 70's but he still recalled our names and those of the family, and many more from down the bottom of the Green. I was grateful to Mr. Powell many years later when I recalled our chat and if it hadn't been for him I would probably had never started this book, for as I knew then and remember now, Winson Green was my World.

Cover illustrations:

Upper: The Railway Inn from Wellington St. - By Ken Storer.

Lower: H.M. Prison, Winson Green. By kind permission of P. Woodbridge.

ACKNOWLEDGEMENTS

I would like to dedicate this to my memory of Mr. Powell and to that conversation many years ago. I would like to thank my wife Margaret for putting up with me whilst I took over the dining room with papers, photos and the typewriter; my aunts, our kid, our Mom without her I wouldn't have been here to have written this book. Family and friends whom I must have bored to death. Alan Dolman and Nobby Clark from down the old end in filling in the gaps with the names of shops and suchlike. A special thanks to my good friends Kay Bates and John Matthews who put all this down, re-typed, sorted out and put it all in order, and my new English teacher Paula (actually my next door neighbour) because without them I would have been lost. This though has been a labour of love from start to finish.

Finally to that man who has put Birmingham well and truly on the map, Dr. Carl Chinn - a true Brummie - for all his help and support, a special word of thanks.

The only German ever to go down Eva Road.
A Heinkel Bubble Car.

Chapter 1
The Beginning

To start this story, perhaps we should look back to the beginning to how my family came together. Everybody must come from somewhere and like all towns and cities the people of Brum formed themselves like a patchwork quilt. Many more learned and glorious men have written wonderful pieces on Birmingham. We can list great notables like Priestley, Baskerville, Feeney, Boulton, the Chamberlains and many more. These were the architects who made our town into a future city.

To develop their practices it needed a workforce of labourers and artisans who came from all over the British Isles to settle here and raise their families. The town encompassed a myriad of individuals, all with different accents and views, but collective in being a part of Birmingham. I make this point because my Grandparents made their way here, and like tens of thousands of others helped weave the tapestry of our city and never went back.

The Smiths
Grandfather was a stationer who came from Chester, while Grandma was from West Derby, Liverpool. She was in service. They came to Smethwick to live in Murdoch Road, by the Soho Foundry, and had four sons, Robert, Arthur, Leslie (my Dad) and Ernie. I never knew my Grandad as he died in 1918. Grandma married again to a James Clark, had another child Alice and took on four other children from his first marriage. I used to find it strange when I was a lad to have one name from my Dad and yet his mother was called Clark. Gran then went and lived in a house on the Smethwick side of Wellington Street next door to the Tizer Pop factory, eventually moving to Avery Road, so in 40 odd years they never moved more than a few hundred yards, and that's where they stopped until both of them passed away.

The Bamfords
Grandad Bamford's family came from Nottingham and settled in King Edwards Road, Ladywood. They had nine children, some of whom were born in Nottingham but Grandad was born a Brummie I'm glad to say. After they got married they lived in Aberdeen Street where Mom and Uncle Bill were born. Granny Bamford was a Maddocks, her Mother and Father came from Derby and

1

they and seven children made the journey to Birmingham on a horse and trap. I often wondered if they carried their belongings with them as well! Mom was born in 1912, the same as Dad. When the First World War broke out and Grandad went away, Granny Bamford move to live with her parents in Wellington Street, on the Birmingham side under the bridge. After the war more children came, Yetty, Mary and Alice (twins) and finally Robert. Uncle Bill died at 43 while supporting the Albion at Nottingham Forest. Ironic to think that his Dad's family had made that journey from Nottingham all that many years previously for him to pass away there.

So now we have the gist of the family and where connections with Winson Green and Smethwick families would come together. We now come to Mom and Dad; you could probably have been able to spit from either of their houses to each other's front door. Dad worked at the Birmid up Smethwick. Mom worked at Nettlefolds as a Press Operator. They were married in 1932 and Leslie was born in 1933. They moved into rooms at Mrs. Brown's at No.1 Eva Road, they then moved into 6/13 before the war, and that is where my part in the proceedings came into the picture.

My Wedding at Bishop Latimer Church, Handsworth New Road
on the 3rd August 1963

Chapter 2
Another Little Brummie

Sunday October 10th 1943 at half past five in the afternoon a big cry came out of the back bedroom, another wartime baby came into the world, whether it was me or Mom first who cried out I'll never know. As I was born 12lb 10oz, was it me for taking a first breath or Mom at the relief of giving birth to a 'three month old baby' as I was always told. Another one with a spout on. Mom and Dad were hoping for a girl but as the old saying goes beggars can't be choosers. To the members of the family present the faces went down, upon which the attendant midwife or sister as they were called proclaimed "if you don't want him, I have a lovely home for boys!" That soon shut them up. By the size of me they were half expecting me to crawl around the bedroom. Aunt Sarah Anne, which we pronounced Suranne (known as Betty to the family) was one of those women all streets had, she helped bring babies into the world, cared for the sick and at the end of their lives, laid them out and placed the pennies on their eyes. She was also present at my birth.

My brother and I

Downstairs were our Dad, Aunt Mary, Aunt Alice (christened Lillian), Aunt Yetty and a cousin who was on leave from the Navy. My brother at that moment in time was in the signal box at the back of the Bamfords. After coming back down the railway embankment to Grandads he was told to go back up home as he had a brother. I suppose he looked at me with great disdain, he would have sooner collected more shrapnel for his tin!

It was at the back end of the war and fortunately the bombing had ceased so I wouldn't have to go into the shelter even

3

though Mom was provided with a respirator for me, and it would be another 18 months before the war was finally over. So that is where my world and life started, over a back yard with an outside lavvy, coal house, miskin and a shared brew house. We were more fortunate than some of my friends who lived in back to back houses and who had to share the lavatory with three other families. Our house was a back house of the villa type with two up and two down, a back yard and a small front garden. When I was growing up I felt very conscious that we lived up an entry, so I used to give my address as 6 Lea Rose Villas as shown on the plaque in between the three houses which made up our side of the entry. There were another three on the other side, which were at the back of number 11, I don't remember the name of their block of houses. Some years ago I went back down Eva Road to have a look at our old house. The communal back yard had been transformed into little individual gardens and the room over the back yard where I was born had been altered into a small bedroom with separate bathroom and toilet. What luxury! No more having to dash over the yard on a cold winters night, but that's another story. A shelter was erected down our end of the yard at the outbreak of the War but only our family used it, as the other two families used to go over to their relatives across Eva Road. Even though the Bamfords had their own shelter down Wellington Street, our Aunt Mary used to come up to our shelter when the raids were on. Also a family from across the road. The family were the Glaziers and were of Italian extraction. Even though they and their parents had settled in this country since the turn of the century, at the outbreak of war they had been classed as aliens and weren't allotted a shelter. The funny thing about is was that he was still allowed to work on the L.M.S. at Monument Road shed! The shelter came down not long after the war was over. There was a small front garden with privet around, but not much else grew in there, not until years later when Dad took an interest in it. The back kitchen was the living room, kitchen and bathroom on a Friday night, while the front room was sacrosanct, it has a three piece suite, occasional table, rugs and of course the piano. This was the 'best' room and was only used on high days and holidays. The front door was hardly opened apart from if Doctor Mackernan called to attend to anyone that was ill. The front gate was opened again only when he was expected. He would knock once on the door, walk through into the kitchen and straight up the stairs. He was a dour man but an extremely good doctor. The front bedroom, when I was old enough, was mine to share with my brother and an uncle. We all slept in one big bed (it certainly couldn't happen today!). My uncle's name is Freddie Collins. He originally came from Summer Lane, he met my Aunt Yetty during the war. They started courting and after the war, due to domestic problems with his own family after he was demobbed he came to live at our house as a lodger until 1955 when he and Aunt Yetty got married. They then moved to Walmley, Sutton Coldfield. I remember him and Uncle Bob in uniform taking me for a walk down Springhill, that must have been about 1947. Things of that age are naturally blurred but I can vaguely remember the 1947 snow, it was like walking through a trench going across the back yard to the lavvy. I remember going on the 32 tram to town (these were eventually withdrawn in 1948.) These are just vague memories like all people have, but I bet all of us remembers starting school . . . .

'Winson Green my world' the corner of Wellington Street and Kitchener Street, Black Patch Park at the back.

Chapter 3
Winson Green the Area

Wynesdon. It seems to conjure up a sleepy middle England village. This wasn't to be. The land was poorly drained, unfit for pasture farming. Owned by the lords of the manor as an open heath, small hamlets were strung along the brook that originated out of Staffordshire. The brook ran down to Hockley, and eventually to power Matthew Boulton's new Soho Manufactory in the late 1800's, probably the largest factory in Europe at that time. To get back to the heath though, we must look to the reasons of Birmingham spreading out from the centre. Up until the 1730's the town limits stopped at Icknield Street on the western side. Parcels of land were owned by wealthy people, such as Sir Thomas Gooch, the lords of the manor and Col. Vyse. Business people wanted more room to build factories and to supply them, it needed people, and the houses for them to live in. So which came first, the chicken or the egg? Well it seemed like the chicken. When Boulton and Watt juniors respectively decided to build a new factory at Smethwick in the 1790's it formed a new boundary for industrialisation. In between, the new Birmingham Gaol was built, alongside the infirmary and workhouse in 1849. After that came the fever hospital. The factories and houses slowly encompassed the area. Winson Green was not the first and only name. Wynesdon was probably the first back in 1327. It changed to Wynnesdon Grene in 1544, to Winson Grene in 1588 and back to Wynsdon Green in 1588, then to Wilsdon green in 1750 and possibly 'Wines Hill'. I must add that gypsies had lived in the area of Black Patch Park for many years. It was in the lea of the area, where the present day Hockley Brook runs. They were still there till after the Great War, but slowly drifted away. Houses were started to be built in the Winson Green area between 1840 and 1890. One instance was the Cornwall buildings in Wellington Street. A builder by the name of James Salisbury who lived in Vere Street bought a piece of land from a Messrs Henry Greatrex and his brother Bertram from Walsall for the princely sum of £900. He then built eight houses on the street and 12 backhouses. This was in 1886. He then sold them to a John Griggs in 1888 for £1000 plus interest, these changed hands twice in the next couple of years. Not bad for such a small parcel of land with so much rent coming in, but lets get back to the story.
Possibly the last of the terrace type properties to be built in Winson Green were

in Beeton Road which was at the back of Bishop Latimer Church, as it is not shown on the 1904 Ordnance Survey. That was the finish of the ribbon of houses in an area which had a border like a dog's hind leg. When I first attempted to write this book, I tried to get any map or reference to borders. I was told that as Winson Green was not a Ward in its own right, we came under All Saints as did Brookfields and Spring Hill, so it was difficult to trace an exact boundary to the Green yet it was easy to define Handsworth from Winson Green as there was the old Great Western Railway line and Hockley Brook. Even though Brookfield had a Birmingham 18 post code they did not class themselves as part of Winson Green. Edgbaston and Ladywood were similar as they had the Dudley Road as a natural boundary, so in my interpretation of this reflects the true borderline of Winson Green.

We need to start at the boundary of Smethwick, which ran down part of Wellington Street into Black Patch Park. There is a drain that runs into the park and runs as an open culvert into another brook that comes from the Smethwick area. They both meet in the park and form the Hockley Brook. So on the western side of the brook was Smethwick and to the east was Winson Green. The boundary ran across Perrot Street alongside the railway line down towards the bottom of Handsworth New Road and then followed the L.M.S. line to the bottom of Bachus Road and up the right hand side of Park Road towards Hockley, then to Hockley Wharf following the canal at a right angle towards the Fever Hospital encompassing Norton Street, crossing over Lodge Road taking in the one side of the hospital and skirting Dudley Road Hospital. People from the Green always reckoned that the hospital was part of our area, those from Brookfields claim it was in theirs. I think they were now correct. The boundary then ran up Lansdowne Street into Aberdeen Street and back up to the Dudley Road over the canal and railway lines and straight down towards Smethwick as far as the Grove Cinema, then back on itself towards Heath Street by Nettlefolds which then went to Cranford Street, Smethwick, back up Heath Street left into Winson Green Road, down the Green into Wellington Street down to the Railway Inn, which was part of Birmingham but shoved its nose into Smethwick, and back to the Black Patch where we started. Because of living on the Warwickshire and Staffordshire border we would have more in common with them than with people from up the Green of down Lodge Road. Kids would have come from Smethwick to attend Foundry Road and Handsworth New Road Schools, we would play together in the park. The area was very much bound together as people would mix, marry and would have families living in the district. The area around there was called Merry Hill and the school was called Sloe Lane which was at the bottom of Wellington Street, but that's another story.

The only factory of any size in Winson Green was Settern and Derwards in Benson Road, they made stationery equipment. My two Aunts, Mary and Alice, worked there until it closed down in the 1960's. People would have to go out of the area at work to places like Chances in Factory Road, Handsworth, Avery's at Soho Foundry, Tangyes in Smethwick and Nettlefolds to name but a few. Metal bashing was the main industry in the area. Around the corner from Avery's was a multitude of large and small factories leading towards Smethwick and probably the largest factory was the Birmid. My Dad worked there until the end of the war. He was an aluminium moulder and worked with men from the Smethwick and West Bromwich areas. So the web stretches further afield. We would have surrogate aunts and uncles from Mom and Dad's friends all over the place.

Apart from Settern and Derwards there were only small businesses in the Green. Apart from working at the institutions (hospital and infirmary), it would have been plumbers, builders, decorators and shop workers.

The employees of the Prison mainly came from outside Birmingham and would live in prison houses that were situated around the prison on the Green and by the school in Handsworth New Road. We had a warder who lived in our street. His name was Whakelam and I remember him to be a huge man, boots gleaming, uniform immaculate, back rigid and his key chain swinging as he made his way down the street. Summer or winter he would carry a mac perfectly folded over his arm. He was a dour man to us kids, he was more like a policeman than a warder. We soon moved quickly out of his way when he came down the street.

My Dad left the Birmid in 1946 when his brother Bob found him a job at the Birmingham Evening Mail in the maintenance department. It was great having a Dad that worked in the town. My brother started work there in 1948 and 20 years later I started there. I think in the end about a dozen of my family worked for the company over a number of years.

When I left school I had to find employment outside of the area and went to Smethwick to work as a bread boy for Birmingham Co-op.

So there we have a brief description of my area. Others might disagree with my idea of the borders surrounding us, but I would argue then, as I would now, with anyone from Handsworth, Brookfields, Ladywood and Smethwick that this was our patch and if I could use a common saying "if you don't like our area, get back up your own end".

Chapter 4
The Proverbial Provident Cheque

All families in our area had the Provident man come around, even though years later they would never suggest that they came to their houses. They certainly did a raging trade up our street. Our Mom was never too proud to admitting to having a cheque every so often. I would be taken to Jeffs on the Dudley Road for new clobber for the yearly rigout. This must have gone on for years, till the one time when I was about 17 when our Mom said to me that she had a "cheque up" and I could get myself a new suit. Off I went into the town, there weren't many stores that took them but Burton's did, so I headed straight down New Street to their shop, in I went to be met by a salesman. "May I be of any help sir?" I told him what I wanted, charcoal grey, roll collar, slant pockets, 16 inch bottoms, duly measured, I felt 10ft. tall, I had never been made to feel this important before in my life, me from a back house down the Green it all seemed so unreal, I felt that I should pinch myself. Then the salesman asked how sir would be paying, would it be cash or personal cheque? I informed him that it would be by Provident cheque, a look came over his face, his accent changed from Edgbaston to Ladywood in an instant, and told me to go and stand in the queue. I looked round there was a long line of blokes all waiting to pay with a 'Provi'. I felt so let down not so much for myself but for our Mom, but a fortnight later when I wend and tried on the suit I felt marvellous. I saw the jumped up snooty git of a salesman using the same flannel on another customer. I wanted to go over and ask how he was going to pay but I thought better of it. That was probably the last time I ever bought clothes with a 'Provi'.

Chapter 5
A Little Bit of Smethwick

As I have said, the Clarke's lived just around the corner from the Bamfords, and the dividing line was Wellington Street. This was an area that I began to grow up in. From Granny Bamfords it was only a stone's throw down to the Black Patch Park. It was handy if I had got dirty playing in the park, I could pop into our grans and have a wash before I went back up home. Me and our Les learned at a young age that you never went home scruffy, unless you wanted a good hiding off our Mom!
Well we need to have another look at the bottom end of Wellington Street. The Bamfords lived in the first house past the railway arches which was on the Birmingham side. Next to them was Doherty's the bookies. In those days they weren't able to advertise themselves as today, it was all cloak and dagger. If someone wanted a bet they would slip up the side entry and go in round the back. Everybody knew it was a bookies, including the police and every so often they would be prosecuted, but I never knew it to be closed down. Next door there was Smelts the grocers then a family called Dix, next door to her was old Mrs. Taylor. I used to play with her grandson Raymond. No matter where we played whether down the park or up the garden he would always keep clean, and me, I would always have to go for that inevitable wash at the Bamfords. Then there was Joyces the hardware shop and on the corner of Wellington Street and Kitchener Street a fruit and veg. a relation of ours, Charlie Wood and his wife kept it for a while. On the opposite corner a pawn shop. Then a row of houses and a chippie. I don't remember the name of the people who kept it. Only that it was a sister of Jack Cutler's, a friend of the family. Those were the days when all they sold were fish and chips or roe and chips. No meat pies, pasties or some of the weird and wonderful delights that they sell today. On a Friday lunchtime it was always packed with people from Avery's. The owner wouldn't serve us with a bag of chips. He was too busy with all the factory workers. That was the extreme end of Birmingham as at that point we were now in Smethwick. I have just mentioned Avery's. It is still there now. To us and our elder generation it was known as the Soho Foundry. Which the name still implies over the entrance. The foundry was opened up in 1796 by Matthew Boulton Jnr. and James Watt Jnr. on land that was more suitable for expansion. The canal having recently been excavated making the movement of goods

easier. Also not having to make do with water power for generation, as at the manufactory at Handsworth, there was also a link up with Murdoch and his invention with coal gas. All of this created a huge workplace which was then sold to a W.T. Avery in 1896 and more factories followed. Grandad Bamford worked there. (I still have his watch that he was given for 25 years service).

Grandad Bamford, Aunt Yetty and friend
outside his house in Wellington Street.

As I was saying Wellington Street was the dividing line. To older people than myself it was called Sloe Lane. There was a school there by that name which most of my previous generation went to. The name Wellington street wasn't used until perhaps the 1880's, as Wellington Street only ran from the Winson Green Road to the bottom of Foundry Road. Even Kitchener Street was a new name it was called Harte Street till about the same time as Sloe Lane changed its name. On the other side of the street were a number of small terraced houses, a couple of shops and a public house by the name of the Engine. As it was in Staffordshire, closing time would be 2.00pm and just up the road on the same side was the Railway Inn, but that was in Warwickshire and they kept open till 2.30pm. As a lad I used to watch the men make their way with a dash up Wellington Street, after the towels had gone on, to get the last drink in the Railway. Next to the Engine was Brindles. They had a typical grocers shop (all scraping a living with so much competition around them) but with a difference. They kept pigs in the back garden. I would take a bucket of peelings round the back of the shop, and they would be mixed in with all the rest of the food. I wasn't old enough to remember them being slaughtered on the premises, only to watch them being taken away, possible to a butchers.

The Engine, Wellington Street in the 1930's.

The shop and piggery were always owned by a Brindle and one of old Mrs. Brindle's daughters Annie married a Luke Stevens. I was told later on that he used to kill the pigs himself. He was one of four brothers, Matthew, Mark, Luke and John and a sister Mary. For a family of possible deep commitment, one of them didn't mind passing the last rites, if only on a poor pig! After the old lady died her son Bob took the shop, and the pigs over and it was to them that I took the scraps. Anyway, lets get back to that side of the street. Next door to the Brindles was Mr. and Mrs. Grainger. They had a daughter called Margaret and we would always be fighting like cat and dog. I used to go over to her house for some fresh picked mint for Sunday lunch. Even though they were friends of the Bamfords I was still charged threepence. Her dad worked for the parks dept. At Christmas time there was always a party at our Grans, and Mr. Grainger would bring his accordion over, but the highlight of the night was when he played the 'saw' a great huge thing which he would vibrate to make a tune with. Only it was always 'The Bells of Saint Mary's' which he would throw himself into with full gusto. He would sway one way then the other till his head would practically hit the wall. Till one night our kid put a pillow up the wall as a joke. It went down like a lead balloon and I don't think he ever played the saw again. Certainly not at the Bamfords.

Grandad Clarke, Aunt Alice, Uncle Ernie, Stan and Reggie Smith.

Next door were the Hodgetts and the other side of the big passage was Mrs. Higgins. She had a shop of some sort. All I can ever remember buying was toffee apples or ice cream, then just above were the Humphries's there were a few more houses and then came the bridge. On the other side of the bridge lived the Healeys. This was just a bit before my time but I still remember the big house. They were well to do. Mr. Healey was in business in making the fat for the preparation of soap. I say "in making", it was in fact boiling down bones. Our aunts called in 'Healeys Unc' I suppose it was a saying for the smell. My Aunt Alice Clarke, Dads step-sister had an uncle that lived at the back of Healeys yard in a shed! and when she was young her and Aunt Alice Bamford would put padding on his half a leg, he would have an old fashioned peg leg and a crutch. I never did see him, he had probably died before I was born, but it never failed to fascinate me. Next to them was the yard where my Dad lived before he got married. Then came a factory which bottled 'Tizer' before it got bombed during the war. That was the end of Smethwick as the border sort of

13

took a right hand turn and went into Victoria Street. I was more at home down that end of Winson Green than probably at the top of Foundry Road. Most likely it was the bag of sucks that Granny Bamford kept behind the pantry door that kept me going down there.

Mom, Dad, Mary and Bobby Bamford

Our Dad, Granny Clarke and two nephews

Chapter 6
Foundry Road - Infants and Junior School

To all children it must be the one day in their lives that they would never forget, I never did. My Mom took me up to the gates, waved to me and told me she would come back to fetch me at dinner time. Miss Moyles who was then the Headmistress, took us into a class room with a large dolls house, rocking horse, building blocks and wooden toys. This was great. For the first week I remember it was wonderful. Then reality stepped in. We were slowly weaned off the toys and introduced to another world of little blackboards and sticks of chalk, no pens and paper yet.

I stopped school dinners for a short time, but played my face up to go home instead. Rationing was still on but our Mom could always find something better. Other children had no option they had to stop. It was probably their only decent meal of the day. As I grew older and mixed with more kids I realised in those days that I was a lot more fortunate than some of the other kids who relied on 'Daily Mail' boots and shoes. Some would come to school day in and day out in the same clothes. I remember one lad would wear a pair of wellingtons throughout the winter and a pair of pumps the rest of the year. Apart from a pair of Mail boots that was his only form of footwear. There was the nit nurse but anything that tried to get into my hair hadn't got a prayer! Mom was a martyr to cleanliness. We had a scrubbed top table in the kitchen and were made to sit on it whilst she start from my head to my ankles with Lifebuoy soap. When it came to my knees it was then the scrubbing brush that came out. I would have been as red as a lobster, but shiningly clean. My brother is 11 years older than me so what he had to endure in the 1930's from Mom I don't know.

The only teachers I can really recall was a Mr. Cross in the Juniors. He was a tall man with glasses and took us for English and I think for other subjects. They say if you can remember a teacher's name they must have made some sort of an impression on you. He did! Mr. Cross was also in charge of the school choir and I managed to get into it. The advantages were that we went to other schools to sing and that day we would not have to do school work. There was a massed choir at the Town Hall from all the schools in West Birmingham and I was picked to go. I think something had gone wrong with my voice because half way through a song the conductor stopped us all then made us sing again.

He must have had fantastic hearing as he picked me out and told me to tell my teacher not to send me again as my voice was too flat. No way! Our Mom had just paid 26 shillings for a blazer and brought four tickets for the show. Well there was only one thing to do, try to hide behind the rest of the kids and mime! The night went off great, our Mom thought I was wonderful and the conductor never saw me. We had another teacher start, a Mr. Parry who took us for lessons leading up to the 11 plus, I failed. I don't know whether it was him or the choir that was my downfall, but I loved that choir.

Then it was time to leave Foundry Road Infants and Juniors and to around the corner to Handsworth New Road Seniors. If I thought the Juniors were hard by God was I in for a shock.

Foundry Road Infants 1949.

Chapter 7
Games and Pastimes

Like all townies, our playground was the street in which we grew up. Whip and Top would probably have been our first game. Hopscotch, both versions, metal hoops with handles attached so you could tazz up and down the road, what a racket they made. Marlies up and down the gutter, seeing how many you could win off your mates. Even better when the glass ones took over the old clays, they were bright and shiny with twirls of colour. Unlike the clays which chipped and discoloured and with the hammering that we gave them we preferred the glass ones.

Cigarette cards and packets were another favourite. We used to flick packets up against a standing packet leaning against a wall. Any packets failing to knock it down would be kept. This would go on till the packet was knocked down and gave someone else a chance to win his packets back. These packets were prized items and the best of the packets we would save, and swop for better or unusual kinds, such as American soft packet types. Cigarette cards were another favourite, they were a real collectable item. The only cards we didn't like were Turf, they were printed on the inside of the packet in blue. I wish I still had some of those cards and packets today. Players with the elaborate drawing of a sailor, an eagle on a packet of Senior Service and a soldier on Greys packets. As we grew older so did the games, hot rice with a tennis ball, it wouldn't half give you a crack if someone was a good shot, bulldog with one standing in the middle of the street and all the rest on the pavement. The object of the game was to all run past him without being tagged, if touched, you would join him in tagging others and so on. We would play these games until it went dark, when you could here the moms coming out and shouting our names to come in otherwise they would send your father after you and you didn't need any further telling.

In the winter it was all football, either up the street or more often than not down the Soaphole, opposite the Railway Inn, a name only known to the kids that lived around there. This was a wide entrance leading to some factories at the back of the railway lines, the name I was told came from an old soap works that was there before the war. In the summer the 'casie' would be put away and the bat and ball came out, no stumps just chalk up against the old shelter at the bottom of Eva Road. The chalk would stick to the ball and prove that you had been bowled out. The ball was a Sorbo, like a hard rubber material and if it hit you at speed it would take pieces out of you.

I remember someone had a pair of old tennis rackets, half the strings were either loose or missing but that did not matter to us, we were all budding Wimbledon champions. We would take a couple of old tennis balls to the Black Patch park and play. Summer seemed to go on for ever. We didn't need theme parks like Alton Towers or Drayton Manor Park in those days we made our own entertainment, we would go out in the morning only returning home when we were hungry.

Train spotting was a pastime I enjoyed as a youngster. At the bottom of Foundry Road were the L.M.S. lines. We would stand at the bottom of the Soaphole, watch for the distant signal to go up and wait with great anticipation to see what was on the Pines Express. You could hear the rumble and feel the vibration as the train came towards us. The gang of us would be waiting pencils and books at the ready. The cry would go up "It's a Jube" meaning a Jubilee type loco, followed by a groan if it was one that we had seen many times before. At the other end of Wellington Street was the Black Patch Park and we would run like the clappers down the street and through the park to the bottom of Perrot Street to catch sight of the trains coming from Wolverhampton to Birmingham Snow Hill on the Great Western line. Mostly they were Castles, green with bright shining brass domes and fittings. My favourite line was the L.M.S. We had an aunt who lived the other side of the entry, her name was Gwennie Mobbley, her husband Harry worked on the L.M.S. and would get free travel passes on the train. I remember once she took me to Tamworth with her two sons John and Paul, from Winson Green Station. That day I saw for the first time a Duchess and City class loco, which we knew better as 'semi's', it was great having this aunt who took me on occasional forays away from the Soaphole.

Me, Gary Smith

I joined the Junior Training Corps., which was a younger version of the Church Lads Brigade. Our kid had been a member some years previous, it was held at Bishop Latimer's Church on the corner of the Handsworth New Road and Beeton Road. We were given a

18

forage cap and a belt. I didn't stay long and joined the Boy's Brigade instead, you still had a forage cap and belt but this time there was a satch which you would have to whiten and keep the brass gleaming. The Brigade met at the Congregational Church opposite the prison gates, our company was the 39th and as far as I was concerned we were the biggest and best. The only envy I had was that the 1st A Company wore a full uniform, all blue, short trousers, blue socks and to top it all a pillar box hat. I suppose in those days all lads wanted to emulate their elders as it was not long after the war and there were still National Service Men wearing uniforms. It was not unusual for young lads to want to wear some sort of uniform, even if their marching was on a church parade. The Captain of our Company was a Mr. Richards, who was assisted by his brother. They kept a hand made shoe shop in Colmore Row, which is now called the Anatomical Shop. I had many good times at the Church. It taught me to be self reliant and I attained badges for many things. Like other young men when we started work and got involved in other pursuits we tended to move away from those youthful activities.

The 39th Boy's Brigade 1951.

Boy's Brigade Camp Exmouth 1957

Bishop Latimer's Detachment Camp 1947.
The Church Lads Brigade. Our kid second from the left at the rear.

Chapter 8
An Aladdins Cave

Growing up after the war, all of us kids wanted to play at soldiers, and there was a place where we could make all our dreams come true. It was Bushells, where for a couple of bob, those dreams could be a reality. Bushells was an ex army emporium, for the want of a better word. The business was run from a large rambling house since pulled down. Between Victor Road and Bachus Road opposite the Mental Hospital in Lodge Road. It was set behind a huge overgrown garden with all the stock behind the house, but lets get to the important bits! What it would have been before the war I don't know, but after it was run by two brothers as a going concern selling ex-war dep't stock, and when I say stock it was immense. Anything from a cap badge to an army three ton truck. For a shilling you could get a Paratroopers helmet, a cap or beret, I even once bought a middle eastern pith helmet. There were shields that were lids off 45 gallon drums with a couple of straps for arm holds, a slit cut out with a piece of coloured plastic inserted in to look out of. We played with these up the street in mock battles with swords and sticks. The only trouble was when somebody gave your shield a clout it sent all your arm numb. We bought sledges that were great long things that we cut in half to use during the winter. All these we could buy for a bob or two. We thought we looked the bees knees in over sized webbing and a hat that was miles too big, marching down to the Black Patch Park to do battle for Queen and country. All this was in future preparation for when we grew older, and to do National Service like our older brothers were doing at that time, but we were not to know that by the time we were their age conscription would be finished.

The 'Para' helmet that I had bought finished up in the coalhouse as a bucket for bringing coal or slack over to the old house. What an ignominious end. As far as I know that helmet was still in the coalhouse when Mom and Dad left in 1971, amongst other odds and sods that were left in that little back house, I often wondered what happened to them. As I said we all wanted to emulate our elders and there was no finer place than Bushells down Lodge Road. It was a veritable Aladdins cave.

Chapter 9
My Mates

I've gone on for so long about the family, the area, school and so on, I think it is about time that I bought my mates into this story. Ronnie Beaman lived in the front houses next to Kershaw's shop and Jeff Hughes also lived in the front houses but next to the big entry to the next set of backhouses up Eva Road. They were my best mates. We would declare undying friendship to each other one minute and the next be scrapping over a cigarette packet that one of us had seen in the horse road. The three of us grew up together, played together in the street and the Black Patch Park and even cycled out of Brum into the countryside and argued together but there was always a bonding between us. Like myself, Jeff had an older brother, David, who was too old to play with us. Ronnie had two other brothers and three sisters and he was the youngest. So coming from a large family there wasn't much for any extras, but like all of us he was brought up, fed well and clothed.

Like I said we all had bikes and Ron coming from a large family had hand me downs so his bike once belonged to his sister Maureen and had no crossbar, but that didn't bother him. We went for miles on those bikes, to Bewdley, Clee Hills and Worcester. This would have been around the mid 1950's. We borrowed a map from Jeff's dad, as he was one of the few people in our street that was fortunate enough to own a car, and with sandwiches and pop in our saddle bags and a couple of bob between us from our Moms, off we would go. I can always remember it being sunny during the big holidays, so we would make an early start. If we were going towards the Severn we would go up Foundry Road, the the Green, into Dudley Road and up into City Road to the Kings Head where we would make our first stop for a drink. Then on through Quinton, down Mucklow Hill, it was great speeding down that hill, but oh the thought of having to ride back up hours later when we were tired, next was through Halesowen and out into the countryside, down the Hagley drag towards Blakedown and into Kidderminster. It seemed odd riding into a large town in the middle of this lovely countryside. By this time we had stopped for a few breaks and the bottle of pop was getting less by the hour. Finally we would reach our chosen destination which was Bewdley. We had left home around 8.00am in the morning and it would be roughly 11.00am when we arrived. What an achievement to come all the way from the Green to here. We would have told anybody if we thought they would have cared to have listened to us. But we felt we were townies and could have done it any time. After cycling up lanes, having a splash in the river, and generally messing about it was time to make our way home. The Hagley Drag was well named. When we came down it many hours before it was a breeze, now it was a real grind. The Obelisk at the top of the hill never seemed to get any nearer and we would end up pushing the bikes to the top. After that it was pretty much plain sailing until we got to the base of the infamous Mucklow. Whatever gears you might have had on you bikes it always was impossible to even go a quarter of the way up it. Anyway after that it as pretty much down hill all the way to the Green. We would arrive home tired, scruffy and very hungry, but it was well worth it. Another journey accomplished and we would talk about it for days after, making it more elaborate each time until we went on our next adventure. However many times we went on these trips, it always seemed so comforting to return to our street after a day out. The three of us were inseparable.

There were other kids we played with in our street, Gwennie Cutler, Dianne Castle, Bob Levy, the Jones twins and the Hamers. By and large we three always stuck together. Yet we all grew up and went our separate ways.

Ronnie moved out of Birmingham to own a village pub, complete with its own green which was used for cricket matches and he would open up the batting for his side. Unfortunately he was only 38 when he died at the crease playing for his side. As a lad he had passed for the Grammar School and went to George Dixons, Jeff and myself failed the 11 plus and went to Handsworth New Road. Jeff at 13 passed to go to Handsworth Tech which left me on my own, but then I met new friends. There was Bob Dollman whose dad kept the garage in Handsworth New Road. His brother Alan still keeps it to this day. I made other friends such as Roy Richards who came to live up Eva Road with his Granny Abasalom who lived at number 10. School mates by the names of Colin Everill, Kenny Banks who came from the bottom of Dudley Road, Mickey Weir, Robert Kerkoff, Dave Moss and many more too numerous to mention but never forgotten. We went all through school together and, as before, we would pledge our friendship and say we would always keep in touch when we left school, but we never did. Perhaps one of these days we shall all get back together, not young faces but greying with glasses.

The three kids who would never grow apart, Ronnie Beaman, Jeff Hughes and myself in the garden of our back house.

Chapter 10
Coronation Day

The weather was overcast and the day didn't augur too well. We had the party up at the local school and then the fancy dress parade around the square just in time for it to start raining, and it didn't half lash down. Afterwards we all went down to the Bamfords. They were one of the few in the area to have a television set. We all crowded into the front room, planks were set across seats, all the kids sat on the floor, the women sat down and the men stood up. I was never so bored but were told to be quiet and watch it. After that it was knees up for the adults. We got fed up of just sitting there so we kids went next door but one to our grans, to George Smelt's who owned a grocers. His son brought out this wonderful record player, it was one of the old fashioned "His Masters Voice" with a great horn. We would keep on winding it up and listening to the music until all of a sudden the spring went and then silence, but not for too long, Mr Smelt came out, the son copped out and we all made quick exits, with the usual cry, "all get back up your own end."

Not to be outdone with being bored, the following week we were all marched up from Foundry Road school to the Regal Cinema which was on the Soho Road to watch The Coronation in colour a week later for the princely sum of sixpence. A fortnight later, we were to go back up there again to watch Edmund Hillary and Sherpa Tensing climb Everest. Wonderful it may have been but it was as interesting as watching paint dry!

These were my recollections of major historical events, I was almost glad to get back to school.

Chapter 11
Handsworth New Road Secondary Modern

What a mouthful our new school was. We knew when we had moved up from Foundry Road that was the easy bit, it was to get us prepared.

Our trip around the corner to the seniors would be different, even daunting. We had been taken there for a day's visit before we broke up for the summer holidays to have a look at our new school where I would spend the next four years. After a luxuriously long summer break I made my way to school. It was a bit of a shock, to put it mildly. Everybody seemed bigger than me, even more so when we were told to keep out of the way of the fourth year boys and of Horace Timbrull and his mates. They were in their last term and he was reported to be the "cock of the school". They seemed like men, but I suppose in a short time when they did leave school they would have to be. We kept our heads down and were ushered into assembly for the usual prayers and a hymn. The Headmaster, Mr. George Liddle, whom we shall discuss later, welcomed us in a fashion and passed us on to our teachers, some of whom had been at the school for many years.

There was one particular teacher, George Berryman, who had been at the school when my Uncle Bob was there is the 1930's and my brother in the 1940's. He was a huge man and could put fear into any pupil. Like most teachers he was handy with the cane and the flat of his hand. He taught the "A" stream and am I glad I was not in his class.

My first teacher was a Mr. Drake who eventually left us in 1957 to teach in Sussex. I bet he found it a bit quieter down there. Then we had a Mr. Parry. He followed us from Foundry Road. We didn't like him there and we certainly didn't like him at the new school. Eventually we got settled into our streams. I tried hard to get into an "A" stream but after one term I was relegated to a "B" stream where I was taught by Mr. Williams, an ex-RAF type with a big moustache. He had the RAF plaque behind his desk which had the inscription "Never has so much . . . . ." etc. underneath. I had a lot of respect for Mr. Williams even though I did receive the cane from him on occasions. He taught English, Art and Music. I still have a couple of books on art that he lent me. I would love to return them. I believe he emigrated to Canada in later years then returned to teach in another Birmingham school which was less salubrious than ours. That's real dedication!

There was one other teacher I shall never forget. His name was Alan Lord, he taught history, geography and current affairs. In history he laid the ground rules from the start. History began in the 1780's with the advent of the Industrial Revolution. Forget about kings and queens and the signing of the Magna Carta, our real history began there. He taught us about the deprivation of the old inner cities and of the hard lives of the population at that time. He made us aware of how we were just as important as a labourer or as a skilled man. After I left school Mr. Lord went on to be a lecturer at Keele University. He must have taught social history. I couldn't imagine him teaching anything else. He was the one who put the feeling for my city into me. I was and still am proud of him.

There were many other teachers who taught at the school who I had no real contact with but still remember. I recall two teachers by the name of Phillips and Byrchmore. The former was short and round and the latter was tall and thin. They always appeared to be in deep conversation and looked an odd couple. We had some great teachers who were like uncles and brothers and others more and stand offish who acted as though they were doing us a favour by teaching us. One thing they all had in common though was they all practised with the cane. I think it was a standard requirement at teacher training college!. The clever ones didn't need it, the fear of it kept you from getting into trouble. Only the teachers who couldn't keep an orderly class resorted to using it at the slightest excuse, but by and large we had decent teachers.

I remember a Mr. Evans who was the metalwork teacher at the annexe which was situated in Queens Head Road, he was probably only 10 years older than me and was more in tune with us. He did not need to resort to the "big stick". Mr. Field the science master, Mr. Huxley for woodwork, and woe betide anyone who didn't get the mortise to fit the tenon, if he didn't clout you his deputy Mathias did. Mr. Taylor taught religious knowledge, but with our class it fell on deaf ears. I remember once we tried to get him to tell us the facts of life, and he started to until we passed comments as kids do. He heard, and that was it. He told us to find out for ourselves. It was the first and last lesson on that subject. I mentioned earlier the Headmaster, George Liddle. He was a thick set man with greying hair and thick glasses. I had been to the Headmasters office on a couple of occasions for the cane. I found out that he was an ex-Birmingham City goal keeper and the year in question, 1956, Birmingham were in the F.A. Cup Final against Manchester City at Wembley. My dad worked at the Birmingham Mail and got me some copies of old photographs of the Blues team of 1931 when they played against the Albion at Wembley and lo and behold the goalkeeper was non other than our Headmaster. I got Dad to get some photographs of the current squad and took them to school and gave them to Mr. Liddle. It might seem like sucking up to the Headmaster, but believe me it was better to get on the right side of him. He even sent for me and gave me a two shilling piece. It was worth it, I never had the cane from him again. I tried that trick on another occasion by entering photo's into the schools photographic competition but it didn't work. I suppose I was pushing my luck by expecting the judges to believe you could take a photograph with a Box Brownie 125 on the byeline of a first division football match!

Summer and winter terms rolled on and the teachers worked hard to try and put something into our brain to enable us to face the big wide world when we left school. Before we knew it we were in our last year of school and we were now "Big Boys', the ones who put fear into the first years, the latter day Horace Trimbulls of the school.

Leaving school photo, Handsworth New Road, 1958 class of 4b.

By now we were going dancing, had girlfriends and even getting into the pictures to watch an X certificate film.

Finally Christmas 1958 came and that was it, the end of 10 years of school. Even the teachers were a little bit different towards us. They knew what it was like outside the school gates and had a better idea of what was in front of us than we did ourselves. The last month passed very quickly, the final term exams were over and we were ready to go. We had our last meeting with the new Headmaster, Mr. Vincent, who was full of encouraging words and wishing us all the best. Handshakes were made all round. Mr. Eden our last term teacher, made us feel not like schoolboys but young men. Time to leave and someone else to take our place. I think I walked out of Handsworth New Road somewhat elated but at the same time naked at the prospect of facing a new chapter in my life.

Chapter 12
Going Shopping

The little shops up the street were the ones that were used really as a last resort, if something had been forgotten or was wanted in a hurry. The little shops were handy for some families as they could have what was referred to as tick or the strap. All of our shopping was mainly done down the flat, the area at the bottom of Lodge Road. We would shop at George Masons. The manageress was a big woman called Connie Timms. I would be sat on the counter as my Gran, Aunts and me Mom did their weekly shop. Sugar was weighed and put into blue bags, cheese cut with the wire and to shut me up Connie would cut a chunk off and give it to me. Bacon would be cut on the slicing machine with a big wheel that would usually be turned by hand and you could have your bacon to what thickness you wanted, which is a rarity these days with standardisation. With all the shopping done we would walk back up Lodge Road to catch the 96 bus in All Saints Street. A sigh of relief would be heard from the women when bags had been put down and a seat was found. That was on a Saturday morning, on the afternoon they would make their way up Main Road apart from my Gran, the morning trip would have been enough for her, to get the extras. There was a Peacocks, a Woolworths, the fruit market and Fosters. The one thing that sticks in my mind about Fosters was the contraption that they put you money in, pulled a chain and a canister went whizzing upwards to some distant office. The bell would ring and your receipt and change would come back. This was one of the few shops that accepted Provident Cheques, another one was Jeffs on the Dudley Road.

I would always know when I was going to have new clothes as Mom would have a 'cheque' and I would be taken up Winson Green Road, into Dudley Road and into Jeffs which was nearly opposite Icknield Port Road. People at times looked down on Provident Cheques but our Mom didn't, nor me. I bought my first suit with one when I was seventeen from Burtons.

In those days shopping was always done locally, people didn't need to go out of their area to shop. Mom would buy all her meat from Billy Rose the butcher, and if it was cooked mead she would go to Albert Newmans. There was a sweet shop by the name of Swans, the Newsagents was Crouches and if you wanted any batteries for your torch there would have been Mrs. Willeys the electric shop, our greengrocer was Tommy Drinkwater. All these shops were in

Foundry Road. In later years I often wondered how they used to make a living. There were three paper shops within a space of a hundred yards, Crouches, Able's and Trickets were in Winson Green Road. There was a confectioner by the name of Clutterbuck who had two shops next to the Congregational Church, that was another lovely name that I shall not forget, one of the Clutterbucks was retail the other wholesale. There was Tommy Wheelers the bike shop, he also sold fishing tackle and second hand model trains! Willey's had another electrical shop on the Green, and when I was a lad I would go and fetch the accumulator, that had been charged up for sixpence for Grandad Bamford on a Saturday afternoon so he could listen to the sports results on the wireless. Fancy carrying a glass container with battery acid by a little metal handle all the way down Wellington Street, another thing which wouldn't happen today.

I used to collect Dinky toys and if I had any money I would go to Dyke's up the Green and would by a model. It would take ages to make up my mind, there were so many to choose from. I wish I still had them today.

After Connie Timms had finished at the George Masons stores, Mom started to use the Co-Op on Winson Green Road. It was a novelty to have the groceries delivered to your house. One of my school mates was a delivery boy for the Co-Op. I remember his bike was bigger than him. Mom, like many others, was a Co-Op member. We had bread, milk and the insurance from the society who came to our door. In those days doors were never locked, the delivery men would come up the entry, knock on the back door, if there was no reply they would come into the kitchen/living room, on the sideboard would be laid out the milk, bread and insurance money, each one would take theirs and leave the "Divvi" ticket, except for the insurance man who would leave his mark in the book.

Christmas time was the magical mystery tour as far as I was concerned. It wasn't like today when it starts in October, it wouldn't get going until December. It all started with Carols at school. The days were very short and it always seemed there was snow in the air. Shops would be decorating their windows out and the great expectancy would suddenly become alive, hints and wishes and wants would be mentioned, but probably to no avail. I remember having a certain amount of pocket money and a bit more from Dad to buy presents for the family. My aunts would take me out, up the Green onto Dudley Road and onto Soho Road, even down to Snapes which was in Great Hampton Row. Snapes was a large chemist that had a huge assortment of talcs, soaps and inexpensive perfumes. I would show my aunts how much money I had and who I had to buy for, the names I shall always remember, Lilies of the Valley, Devon Violets and Lavender Water. I would go to our Granny Bamfords and wrap them up and write little cards and hope they were doing the same for me.

The smell and feel of Christmas would be all around, birds would be hung up outside the Butchers, and nuts, dates and tangerines would appear in the green grocery shops. The newsagent would be advertising for Wills Whiffs. December was a magical month, holly and mistletoe would appear at the market on the Soho Road. It didn't matter what the weather was like, Christmas was coming. I suppose nothing much has changed today except it starts two months earlier and has gone from hoping for a 26" second hand bike to the state of the art computer. However, I am not knocking this, I would have wanted something better.

After Christmas was over it would have been back down the flat and start the year all over again. On high days and holidays we would have gone down the town with Dad, more often than not if he had a Saturday off. We would get off the 96 bus at Edmund Street and down Hill Street through Elizabeth Drive to the back of the market hall. It was all open then as the bombing had blown the roof off during the war, but it didn't take anything away from the atmosphere. Fresh fish, shell fish and crabs were laid out on slabs, butchers selling prime cuts of meat. All competing with one another. Our Dad bought me my first tortoise from out of there I think it cost him half a crown. At the tope of the steps was a sea mine I put pennies in on tip toes, and later on bending down to do the same. There was the old lady at the bottom who used to sell brown paper bags, only a Brummie or someone who used to visit the market would remember that voice "Andy Carrier" and the newspaper sellers shouting "Spatch or Mail" it went through you like butter.

The Bull Ring was a mass of people milling around the two rows of stalls that started from the top by High Street, down the Church of St. Martin's at the bottom. I remember the Bible Preachers who used to get the crowds going and the escapologist who would remarkably get himself out of sacks and chains. The area from the top of the market where Times Furnishing was, had been bombed and some shops had been built in prefab style. One of these was Keelings, the pet shop, which also sold fishing tackle. I guess I would have been about nine when Dad took me there to buy some fishing tackle. He told me many years later that he had spent 26/- and I had a kreel, rod, reel, net, floats, hooks and line. I never really remember asking him for it but was forever grateful. Today it wouldn't buy 50 metre of line. This was Brum's original market. Steeped in history. Every market trade in the middle of town, but never to be the same since people were driven below ground level for the car to be king. Even the statue of Nelson was moved for the road. Surely the next time round they will get it right.

The town was a maze to me, but Dad knew all the short cuts as he had worked in the town since the war. As I grew older I began to find my way around. It seems wrong in retrospect but I shall never forgive the way in which the City fathers ripped the guts out of the middle of Brum.

Off High Street was Union Street. I say was, because it was a street on its own, unlike Martineau Street which has been reduced to a square. Union Street radiated down to the bottom of Bull Street opposite which was Albert Street and Dale End. I brought my first Teddy Boy clothes from Zissmans on the corner of Bull Street and Dale End. I know times must change but why with so much ferocity as happened in the centre of Brum? The Exchange buildings on the corner of New Street and Stephenson Street have long gone and many more too. Debenhams, the Beehive, Lewis's have all disappeared, long live the memories of a past pleasure of shopping in Birmingham. The vast number of people still use their local areas to shop and still go into town, but to me I seem to look behind the concrete and remember what it was like.

Victoria Square, Birmingham in the 1950's

Chapter 13
Days Out and Holidays

The earliest recollection I can remember was going to Blackpool to see the lights and the tower. We also went to Leamington to see their illuminations, which were rather disappointing because there was no sea front! Just a park to walk through. Other trips would be to the Lickeys, down to the town on the 96, a short walk down Hill Street to Navigation Street then wait for the tram in a long queue. The tram would run down John Bright street into the Horse Fair, trundling along Bristol Street into the Bristol Road, up through Selly Oak ,through Northfield and on to Rednal. The tram would come to the terminus at the Lickeys run around a big circle and face the way back to Birmingham. After getting off the tram we would make our way up to the hills. It was a big family day out, Mom, Dad, Aunts Mary and Alice, Uncle Fred and Aunty Yetty and of course Gran and Grandad Bamford. I would always have my mate with me, Jeff Hughes. When you came from the Green it was like another world to visit the Lickeys, even the grass in the Black Patch Park had a tinge of soot on it from the factories around. The Lickeys was open country as far as I was concerned.

On Sunday after dinner our Uncle Bob would come and take me out, it would always be a train ride, sometimes to Sutton Park or to Tamworth, but it was the main holidays which were the highlight of the summer. I was one of the lucky ones in that our Dad had a regular job at the 'Mail' and also an evening job at the theatre. Holidays were always the last two weeks in August, we would start getting ready at least a month before. We always went by train. I would be woken early on the Saturday morning to have a cup of tea, while Mom made sandwiches and a flask for the journey. Dad would have already made some bacon and egg sandwiches to eat when we got on the train. Off we would go, catching the bus from the terminus at the bottom of Wellington Street, tired but excited as we would either make our way down Edmund Street to Snowhill or down Hill Street to New Street Station. Either way it was magical, standing on the platform waiting with hundreds of other holiday makers. Adults were jockeying for positions and the rumble of the locomotive approaching the platform, the steam and the smoke as it passed by, the squeal of the brakes and the rattle of the buffers as the train came to a halt, then it was every man or woman for themselves, but they always made sure the kids got on first, a rush to find a compartment and better still if it had a table. Cases on racks, coats off and settle down for the journey. As I said before I enjoyed train spotting and Dad would buy me the latest Ian Allan train spotters book at Menzies at the station and I would be writing down numbers whenever I saw a loco. If we went to Margate we would change at Euston, and we would spend some time in London before going to Victoria. The colour on the train would change from red to green and another spotter's book, and it wouldn't be long before the sea came into view.

The railway station at Margate was next to Dreamland the main fun fair. Mouth drooling I was told to forget it as we had to get to the guest house first. In those days there were always kids outside of any seaside station with mokes to take your cases to your destination for a few coppers. We always stopped at Mrs. Barnes who had a guest house in Cliftonville. No ensuites in those days but a bowl and large jug, which was filled with hot water in the morning by the landlady.

I couldn't wait to get out of my clothes and put on some shorts, tee-shirt and pumps and get down to the beach. After much pleading, off we would go. It seemed the holiday would go on for ever until Mom would start packing towards the end of the second week, and then it was over for another year, but never forgotten.

Muddiford 1952

Chapter 14
Never at 'Um'

The times that I head our Mom say that. I never really understood till years later, then the penny dropped. After the war as I have said earlier, Dad went to work at the Evening Mail and a chap named Les Wadley went to work in the machine room, he worked part time at the Theatre Royal in New Street and asked our Dad if he fancied a part time job there. Our Dad wasn't one to say no, and so he started at the theatre, his job at that time was in the 'Limes' right up at the back of the 'Gods' the highest point in a theatre where the main spotlights were shone onto the stage. He partnered a man by the name of Dennis Cooper, whom I shall tell of later, who then went backstage as chief electrician. Dad then had a new partner by the name of Harry Cauldwell. They were to remain good friends for many years. His proper job was for Davenports the brewery as a home delivery salesman. The Royal, as a grand theatre, had stalls, dress circle, circle and upper circle which I have said were the 'Gods'. I would sometimes go down to the theatre, and as I knew all of the security men would be able to make my way up to see Dad. The climb seemed to go on forever till I eventually arrived at the back of the last row. When looking down to the stage it looked so steep that it felt that one slip and you would tumble all the way down onto it. Up through another door, up another staircase and into a tiny room with three huge arc lamps, Dad and Harry were there guiding those lamps, through a window I watched as they followed a dancer or singer across the stage with the spotlight. I once was allowed to try my hand, but I made a fluff of it, at once the internal telephone rang and it was Dennis Cooper wanting to know what was going on. I was never given the chance again. Apart from Sundays I never got to see Dad much, he would be out in the mornings before I got up, and in at night long after I had gone to bed. On a Saturday night after the last performance he would do a 'get out' taking out the previous weeks scenery and props till the early hours of the morning and sometimes follow it on by getting the next show in, not getting home till Sunday afternoon, then having his dinner and go up to bed, up about seven o'clock wash and a change and down the Railway Inn.

The Royal closed down, and was demolished in 1956, and Dad went into semi-retirement until Dennis Cooper, who by that time was chief electrician at the Hippodrome, got in touch and asked Dad if he fancied another part time job as his number two as a stage electrician. Mom probably thought that he had got it out of his system but of course she was to be proved wrong, and in the winter of 1957 Dad once again walked through a stage door and took up again another part time job in the theatre. He never worked the 'Limes' again, he worked back stage as a stage electrician in charge of floods, pageant lamps and any other sort of electrical stage apparatus, and back to 'get outs' and 'get ins'. This I suppose went on for perhaps another 10 years or so, till our Mom finally had her way and he packed up the theatre. Not only did he do that, but he was a runner for a bookies down Springhill. He'd collect bets from the Mail with a fellow called Billy Lomas and take them down there in his dinner hour, come back into the town and have a couple of pints and a sandwich in the Old Contemptibles in Livery Street. Then back into work at the Mail in the publishing room. People said he was a workaholic. I just think he enjoyed it. I worked with him in the theatre in the early 60's and once again in 1968 when he got me a job at the Mail. He was a fantastic bloke and I missed him dearly when he died. It was in his blood to keep on the go, but I can understand our Mom saying 'yer father, were never at um".

Chapter 15
All Areas have their Characters

After the war and the 50's came, work was more settled. Unemployment was dropping and a spirit of optimism was setting in. More money was available, the hard 'thirties' had gone, men had changed jobs and characters who had survived by their wits and standing in society were being replaced by a new breed of men. Some of the old timers had remained, but now they sat down at the 'Sons of Rest' in Black Patch Park and Summerfield Park and canted to us kids about what it was like in times gone past. (I wish there had been tape recorders and camcorders in those days). But as I have said before we were too full of ourselves in growing up to be listening to our grandads.

Possibly of all the well known characters in the area had gone by the time I was growing up. The trams had finished in 1948 on our route but we had a local character by the name of Goode who drove the tram when it was illuminated for special occasions and also the last tram from Wellington Street back to Rosebury Street garage. My Dad, our kid and Freddie Castle travelled on the last tram back to the depot where it was systematically stripped down to its chassis by collectors and anyone else there that wanted a piece of the last 32 tram. Dad and Freddie Castle had carried a seat all the way down the Soho Loop Canal which eventually finished up in his pigeon loft. A hanging strap was cut down and given to our kid, much to his dismay it was left at the old house along with his tin of shrapnel when Mom and Dad left in the 70's.

When I was a kid I remember hearing about a man who had no legs, his only form of travel was on a trolley. He lived in Villiers Street and evidently when he wanted to get onto a bus he would wait at the stop, when the bus came he would haul himself on the platform by swinging himself up by the pole and hauling his trolley up behind him. He would remain on the platform until it was time for him to get off and do it all in reverse.

There was another character who lived in Foundry Road and she kept a haberdashery shop. Her name was Mrs. Bird. I am told everything in the shop was a jumble of material and clothes and when you went through the front door she would have to clamber over clothes, boxes, bags and possible the counter.

At the bottom of Eva Road there was a shop straight opposite Foundry Road. It was a newsagents and owned by a Mrs. Richardson. The shop was all a jumble and when fresh papers and comics were brought in they were just put on top of previous ones and so on until the counter was piled high. I suppose every so often there would be a clear out but I can always remember it being that way. To me, as a kid, it was always a surprise that she could find that weeks Dandy or Beano but she did. Our Dad helped to clear out the shop when the old lady died. There was money in between magazines, papers, pop bottles and sweet jars. Papers and magazines that were ages old. She probably did not know how much she was worth. To find a shop like that today would be a collector's paradise.

Pawn shops were becoming a thing of the past, perhaps because money was more plentiful and people didn't feel they needed to take their goods to 'Uncles' but I remember one that was on the corner of Perrot Street and Foundry Road by the name of Bartons. It was right opposite to Goode's the tram driver who also kept a shop in Foundry Road.

We had a character who lived in Perrot Street, to us she was known as Lottie, and her surname was Dix. The story was that she had been left by her husband and had gone a bit eccentric. We used to taunt her although we didn't know why, I think it was just for the thrill of her racing out of her back door and chasing us off. It was a dare to go down her back entry and shout names. she would often chase us with anything at hand. We would jump over a big wall that dropped at the back of our house in Eva Road. It was about ten feet high, but with Lottie closing in on you, you would have jumped off a mountain to get away.

On a Sunday the pig man would come around for scraps. He had a horse and trap, and kept a piggery up the wicket by our Granny Clarkes. His name was Vic Brookes, and at Christmas we always had a nice bit of pork from him. Mind you we could smell Vic coming three streets away from the smell of those bins on the back of his trap.

Also on a Sunday I always had a treat, penny winkles, from a street vendor who would push his handcart up to the Railway Inn at the end of his round. He would sell shell fish and salad outside the pub. Dad would come up home for his dinner slightly merry with a bag of winkles for me which cost 6d and a bag of celery for him and our Mom. They knew it would keep me quiet, because all afternoon I would be busy with a pin.

Authority was always in the forefront in those days from anybody in uniform. Whether it was a nurse to a copper, or the manager of the Winson Green Cinema. His name was Hall and inside the picture house he was gaffer. If he thought you had been in too long and seen the programme through he would flash the light up the row and finger you out and escort you from the Cinema. We had our own back on a Saturday afternoon, when we would go to the matinee, one would pay to go in and when the lights had gone down and the film had started one of us would slide down the side aisle and open one of the panic doors that opened into Wellington Street. We would let the rest of the gang in, one at a time. We weren't the only ones to do it, as other kids from off the Green were doing it as well. You never knew when you opened the door who you were letting in and how many.

We used to have a policeman come around to our school and speak on road safety. His name was Sergeant Rutter. The stories of him abounded. It was said he dived off a bridge into a canal at the back of Averys to save someone. In reality now he must have dived 20 feet into the cut that was only 4 feet deep! But he still remained our local hero.

Vicar Smythe was the vicar of Bishop Latimer's. The name conjures up a staid pillar of the community which he was of course, but he was also a character. He was a brilliant man to talk to and very educated, but he liked a glass of bitter. He was a regular in the passage at the Railway Inn in Wellington Street. He was a good conversationalist and domino player! The week before we were about to get married Vicar Smythe was taken ill. On the Saturday of the wedding his wife came to me at the Church just before Margaret (my bride) had arrived to tell me that he had not recovered and was unable to take our wedding ceremony. She assured me that everything would be alright as there would be a stand in. The cleric turned up in his gown. I remember him as bald headed and bespectacled and then found out that he was the Chaplain to the prison. The service over, we went to sign the register in the vestry. I realised then that he would put down all the relevant details on the marriage certificate but to see 'D. Williamson, Chaplain to H.M. Prison, Winson Green' on paper was a bit of a shock to say the least. This I understood happened for the next couple of weeks. So perhaps it makes us, along with a few other couples, unique. Vicar Smythe died not long after that. Another face, another character gone.

Chapter 16
Down the Town

To outsiders it is a city, to a Brummie it is the town. We never talked about going into the city, it was always 'going down the town'. As a kid it was a special treat to know that you were going down the town with our Mom or Dad. Sometimes without them knowing, us kids would scrape up the bus fare, a penny ha'penny, just to ride on the 96 into the town and pay the same fare to come back without getting off. It was wonderful, almost adventurous, seeing the rows of terraced houses and factories pass us by, the large railway yard on the Great Western at Hockley, the clock at the top of Warstone Lane in the Jewellery Quarter, the hustle and bustle would become greater as we came up Summer Row and into the town, the buildings would be huge and very grand looking we couldn't wait till we grew older and get off that bus and go into the town. Then we did grow older and were finally allowed to go on our own. We would get off at the terminus in Margaret Street and walk through Eden Place. On one side was the Bank of England the other the council house, there was a man who drew on the slabs with chalk. People would stop, look and possibly admire and throw coppers into his cap. He would never look up but just kept on drawing. At the end of Eden Place the area would open up into Victoria Square. To the right Galloways Corner, an imposing Victorian building that swept round into New Street with shops at ground level and offices above. This was the start of the adventure into the town. To the left Colmore Row with all the banks and institutions. It was the financial heart of Brum, and in the streets off Temple Row and Bennets Hill there were solicitors offices with men in dark jackets, pin striped trousers, bowler hats and the proverbial rolled umbrella. At the end of Colmore Row lay the old Great Western Station, a lot grander than the one that resides there today. On the corner of Colmore Row and Snowhill a man sold small bags of baked potatoes. No butter or fillings in those days, just a pinch of salt! Opposite there lay Steelhouse Lane and right on the corner was Harrisons the opticians, I remember a large neon sign of a penguin with glasses on. As today the old law courts and the police station on the right hand side but on left where the Evening Mail offices are, were small shops and little factories, further down, the old General Hospital. Beyond that was the Castle Pub, notorious we heard, for Yanks visiting there during the war, and ladies of a certain character. Nearby was a large roundabout in front of the

Fire Station. Dissected by tram lines for trams to go straight across, this was long before the flyover for the 38M. It was as far as we got down to that end of the town and it was back to the centre where we wanted to be. We would go back to Bull Street. To the right Greys and to the left Lewis's, the finest shop ever as far as I was concerned, to walk up to the top floor and look over the balcony right down to the basement, then out of Lewis's and down into Lower Bull Street on the left hand side was Macfisheries it was on the corner of a little side street, up that side street lay other little shops. One in particular was Thomas's the wine and spirit merchants who sold it loose from the barrel. They later moved down opposite Moor Street Station where the old Evening Despatch buildings were, but having come out of the middle of the town were not as successful and finally closed down. At the bottom of Bull Street was six ways made up of Martineau Street, High Street, Albert Street, Dale End and New Meeting Street, from there we would make our way down to the Bull Ring, there is only Marks and Spencers there now, no Co-Op, no News Theatre or Times Furnishing to name a few. When we had walked through the Market Hall we would come into Worcester Street and into Queens Drive, the thoroughfare which divided the old Midland railway and the L.M.S.

The smell of smoke and steam stayed with me forever. In Hill Street there was a pub called the Malt Shovel which was partially bombed during the war, only the public bar was left. Later it was knocked down for an upmarket pub to be put up in its place. That eventually was to be closed down and yet another opened up. They should have left the old one standing at least it had some history behind it, if only for being half bombed! Straight up Hill Street was the old General Post Office, but we would walk into Stephenson Street past Pinfold Street, Lower Temple Street and Burlington Arcade. On the left was the best book shop in Brum, Hudsons, up on the right was the old New Street Station. At that time it was the only open main line station in the country to have no platform ticket machines. A train spotters paradise! This was made possible as there was a public right of way between Stephenson Street and Station Street up into New Street. This area hasn't changed much over the years only possibly the change of ownership of the buildings. At the bottom of New Street was Marshall and Snelgroves, possibly a former Rackhams in all its previous glory. It's now gone. It closed down as did many well known businesses such as The Midland Educational, Yates' Wine Lodge, Pattisons in Corporation Street, the Kardomah in New Street, these are just a few. There were the main thoroughfares but there were numerous alleys, and rat runs. You could go through one door of a shop or pub and out into another street, that hasn't changed much but it seemed a lot more exciting then, and that is how it made up my town centre, I could go on and on but Brum has never stopped still. Nor should I want it to.

Chapter 17
Earning a Copper

If you wanted any money of your own, you had to work for it by running errands for family or neighbours and hope they would be generous. Or else you could get a part time job. The most obvious being a paper boy. Other kids did it so why not me? One of the Bradshaws who lived at the back of Trickets the paper shop opposite the prison on Winson Green Road, told me the owner wanted a lad for a round. I got the job. I never realised how heavy papers were and how far you would have to walk. I thought running errands was bad enough but carrying that great bag stuffed with Evening Mails and Birmingham Despatch's down Lodge Road then starting the round, Don Street, Musgrave Road, Devonshire Street, etc., they seemed to go for ever.

Fortunately it was an evening round because I couldn't face that lot in the mornings as well. Saturday was collecting day. As well as delivering the papers you would have to collect the money, including payment for the morning papers that were delivered by somebody else, then get back to the shop to settle up. I could earn an extra bob in taking the Sports Argus' over to the jail for the prison officers, but that was down to luck of the draw and who Mrs. Tricket wanted to go. Sunday would come round too quickly and at some god awful hour I would have to get up to take the Sundays. It was a different round but just as hard, I would have to go back to the shop for a second bag. It felt as though everybody would have three papers. The round was not too bad though, Villiers Street, Franklin Street and Wellington Street and for all that I got 7/6d a week. After the Sunday papers were finished I would get back home, have some breakfast, get changed to go to the Boys' Brigade for church service. I was always getting told off for falling asleep during the service, but what could you expect after delivering all those papers. I also used to help our coalman load up coal from the coal wharf, which was situated on the Old Great Western line up the 'Distructer' (the proper name was Queens Head Road,) another local name which at that time I never could figure out. My aunts worked at Settern and Derwards in Benson Road and I got to know a lad whose mother worked with the girls. He worked part time in the Jewellery Quarter. His name was Colin Muddiford I wonder if he eventually worked in the trade? We worked for a jewellers in Vyse Street, they mostly worked in marcasite rings and brooches, for around 12/- a week. It was handy working in that area as you could catch the 96 bus around the corner from the school and be in the quarter by half past four. This would have been around 1957 and I found another job in Northampton Street off Hall Street for a firm of enamellers called Collins's for another three shillings a week. Anybody that worked in the quarter before it was re-developed would know what I am saying. They were all old premises enlarged and altered to accommodate whatever trade that were being produced there. This was no different at Collins's. It never ceased to amaze me how much work was turned out in such a confined space. Dust was a major problem in the enamelling shop and my first job was to sprinkle the floors with water before I swept up. This I learned the hard way on my first day as I swept up with no water and caused such a fog of dust. I didn't half get a telling off. After that I made sure I filled up an empty bottle with water when I first went in. Even in such cramped conditions everybody seemed happy enough. I used to watch the women applying enamel to the badges at such a rate with a multitude of colours. They produced car badges, medallions, club badges and almost anything that needed enamelling, Collins's would do it.

I was about to leave school at that time and was looking for a job, I didn't fancy working at Collins's though. I was quite good at art at school so I fancied something artistic. I heard of a job going in Hall street at a silver engravers. I had an interview and the owner was pleased with my work so he offered me the job as an apprentice in silver engraving. I asked him what my wages would be, because our Mom had told me to, and it would be 30/- (£1.50) and pay my own stamp which was 2/6, this would be a six year apprenticeship. I then went home and told Mom what I had been offered, she didn't want to know. She said my brother brought that home years before and I had to get a job that paid better. Mom said the Co-Op Bakery at Messenger Road in Smethwick wanted bread lads, she must have found this out from our baker and told me to apply for a job. There was no argument, I had got to bring home more money!

So after the shortest of Christmas holidays I started at the Co-Op. There was a week's training of sorts into the aspects of working for the Co-Op at the main offices in High Street in the centre of Birmingham. I didn't mind that, the hours weren't bad, and it was great to travel into the town. The Bull Ring hadn't been re-developed then and at lunch times I would go out and have a mooch down there and around the town in general. However, the following week was a different story. I was up at six o'clock on the Monday morning and made my way to Smethwick. It was a cold January morning and the thought of that walk didn't fill me with much optimism for my future working life, but when you had to go, you had to go! It was pitch black dark when I left home, out of Eva Road, down Foundry Road past the Railway Inn into Victoria Street up the wicket that ran alongside the railway embankment, past Murdock Road and Avery Road, where Gran and Grandad Clarke lived, up towards Avery's over the railway lines that ran into the back of the factory, along the canal up and over the foot bridge that spanned the railway goods yard at the back of Tangyes, up Alma Street, past the Crystal Palace pub across the road into Oldfield Road and into the Bakery yard. The walk was about a couple of miles and if it were raining I'd get soaked before I had got to work and started my round. I could have used a bike, but I would have had to go all around the wrekin! On my first day I had to report to the Bakery foreman, his name was Dangerfield, he was a friendly chap if you never got into trouble or were not persistently late. He allocated us to different roundsmen and all of a sudden you realised you were no longer a boy and that you had stepped into a mans world and had to get used to it fast.

For a few days I was put with different roundsmen as a spare lad, and eventually one of the checkers a Mr. Ratcliffe took me to Quinton to work with a roundsman whose lad had not turned in. His name was Eric West, he seemed an irascible bloke, but as the years went on he turned out to be a very good friend.

My first week was over, it had been only a matter of weeks since I had been going to school and earning a few bob from part time jobs to working a 44 hour week in all sorts of weather. I picked up my first week's wages in a little brown packet. I took it home unopened to Mom and after she had checked it I looked at the pay slip. For all that work I had picked up two pounds four and nine. Mom gave me the 14/9 and put the thirty bob in her purse, that was for my board. I was three pence worse off for I were getting 15/- a week part time, it didn't seem fair somehow but that was life.

I mentioned earlier that at school I was good at art, well my brother was going to get me a job in the process department of the Evening Mail. To get as far as that I needed to go to the Printing College in Margaret Street. I took my work and exam results to the principal and he seemed satisfied with me, all that was left was for me to have a simple colour test. I failed. I was fourteen and it seemed that the bottom of my life had fallen out. I caught the 96 bus out of Congreve Street in tears. I didn't even get a chance to get to the Mail at that time.

I had been working at the bakery for a few months when my brother got me an interview at a printers down Livery Street. I met the print manager and went through the same rigmarole again. He seemed very keen until I told him about my colour blindness. He told me what I already knew anyway, that I would not get the job. Although they were only printing black and white at that time they would eventually move to four colour and there wouldn't be a job for me. Apologies were given and he wished me all the best for the future. So back to the bakery. I never bothered trying again in being a printer, but I do regret not having the opportunity to be a silversmith.

Many years later, however, I did start work at the Mail and have spent 30 years in the print trade at different print houses. Ironic isn't it.

My Dad apart from working at the Mail used to work part time at the Theatre Royal in New Street before if was demolished in 1954 and then at the

Birmingham Hippodrome. He preferred the Royal as he classed it as the premier theatre of Brum, home to most opera and ballet companies. After the Royal it only left the Alexandra Theatre and the Hippodrome, the former for plays and musicals and the latter for variety. Later the Hippodrome began to have more of a mix of shows, unlike today when it is the home of the Birmingham Royal Ballet Company and top shows that visit the city. It was then that I started to work part time there in 1960, six shows a week for 54/- (£2.70), extra for 'get outs' (taking the old show out of the theatre and ready to bring the following one in). The first night when Dad took me back stage was wonderful, to see actors and actresses that you only ever saw on TV. I must have been standing there open mouthed until Dad said "come on you've got work to do, not to stand around watching the show." In all the years he worked at the theatre he was never overawed by the surroundings, where as me and our kid would have worked back stage for nothing. Dad was a back stage electrician, but could turn his hand to anything. Working at the theatre has stayed with our family, my brother and his sons work back stage at a large theatre in Llandudno. I worked plays, reviews, pantomimes and even an opera, 'Orpheus in the Underworld'. The shows that I liked best were the varieties. I remember Ken Dodd and his show in 1960, he was as barmy then as he is now. Rock and roll was very much at the fore with us and it was magic being back stage when some of my idols were a few feet away on stage. Eddie Cochrane, Gene Vincent, Billy Fury, Joe Brown, Lonnie Donnigan, Marty Wilde and lots more. What wonderful times.

Scribban's Canteen

45

Chapter 18
Growing Up and Going Out

With a few bob in your pocket after a weeks work, we would be ready to go out. Now we had left school we felt like adults. There was only one difference, we still had bum fluff around our chins, but that didn't matter. We could afford new clothes, we did not, as yet, frequent pubs as we preferred coffee houses. Nott's Cafe at the end of Thornhill Road by Handsworth Park, the Milkbar on the Flat, the Elsombrero down the Horsefair, the Volcano at the end of Hingeston Street, these were some that we used to go to. They all had juke boxes, but in those days they played 78's. When selected they would drop onto the turn table with such a bump I'd always wondered why they never broke, these were later to be phased out and 45's were in. We would pour loads of tanners into those machines. The cafe owners must have made a fortune. We would drink coke from the bottle, copying the American youth that we saw at the pictures. That was another form of pleasure, knowing now that we could get into see A and X certificate films, even better still if you could take a girl in with you. We were still a little gang and it was hard to find three or four girls on their own, but if you clicked on your own the rest would understand.

There was only one other way for all of us to get a girl and that was to go dancing. I had been going to the Ninevah Dance Studios before I left school, it was run by George Last and Dorothy Careless and they taught up to gold medal standard. I got to a bronze, but before long rock and roll dancing overtook the formal ballroom stuff for most of the night, much against the wishes of the purists, but that was up to them. We only lived for rock and roll. For us to look smart to go dancing we'd need fashionable clobber. There was Zissman's in the town or Grooms in Windmill Lane, Smethwick. The real Teddy Boy era was finishing but the drainpipe trousers were still in, cutaway collars were the new fashion with still a hint of Teddy Boy gear. The old chap didn't like it and wasn't very happy when I had 18" bottoms cut down to 14's.

Saturday nights we would get dressed up and I would spend half an hour in front of the mirror making sure the quiff was perfect, and then out like a rat up an entry to meet the rest of the gang, and up to the Ninevah, have a good night and if lucky take girl home. We met plenty of new friends there. One was a Mickey Tallett, he was a great lad and the only one with transport. He had an Ariel Arrow motorbike and we would take it in turns to ride pillion back home.

Unfortunately Mickey was killed just outside Bridgnorth. It was a tragedy as he was an only boy and his dad was going to buy him a car on his 17th birthday. He was cremated at Perry Barr Crematorium. Six of us carried his coffin, we all wore black. Mickey would have been proud of us. His pillion passenger, another mate, Terry Yates was thrown off and survived. He also was one of the pall bearers, but that gang wouldn't get back again as it was.

Another one to join our crew was Benny Brain who's father owned Brain & Son the undertakers. He lived on the Warwick Road, Solihull. I never asked him how he came to use the Ninevah. We went to his house one Saturday night, he met us at the railway station just around the corner from where he lived. We walked up the Warwick Road and turned left into what I thought was another road only to find it was their drive. The entrance hall was bigger than our front room. I never thought that anyone that I would ever know could live in a house that big. It was like nothing I had ever seen before, two bathrooms, mind you we had two bathrooms at our house there was the tin bath that came from across the yard to go in front of the fire on a Friday night, and when I got older the public washing baths in Bachus Road. We stayed that night at Benny's as his Mom and Dad were away. If we wanted to we could have helped ourselves from their drinks cabinet, but as I have said we weren't into proper drinking. We had taken some girls with us from the dance studio and we were going to come home on the last train, but by the time we realised we had left it too late, one of the girls rang up her Dad to say that she and her sister were going to stop overnight with the other girls. Her Dad was to have no cotter with it and he came all the way from Handsworth to pick up all the girls and to let us make our own way home the next day. He must have thought we were daft enough to think he would let these girls stop there with his blessing. I will not mention the girls names for any embarrassment it might cause them, but as true Winson Green lads, hands on hearts ,they would have been safe with us!

The Ninevah studios were on the corner of Bachus Road and Soho Road over the top of Broadmeads the television shop. One night there was an accident and a car ploughed into the shop and made the whole building unsafe. The dance studio moved to a large hall at the end of Grove Lane and Oxhill Road. We kept going for a while until we found another place in Austin Road, just off the Holyhead Road. Other people started to drift away as we missed the old studios. I tried other dance halls like Laura Dixons in the town, Hawleys on Dudley Road and the Casino in Corporation Street, but it was never to be the same.

Chapter 19
Leaving the Gang Behind

That little bit of time between leaving school and finding a regular girlfriend, wasn't too long in my case. Up until I was 17 I had been going out with me mates, nothing else changed at that point. When I started to work for the Co-Op I took a latent interest in sport again. I joined the bakery cricket club which was based at Barrows Lane Sports Ground Yardley, and was owned by the Co-Op. We played all over Birmingham against different works teams in the Wednesday afternoon league. At about the same time I took up judo. I joined a club that was up the Queens Head Road just up from the cafe on the corner of Alexandra Road. It was a large wooden building at the bottom of a long overgrown garden and had I not been shown where to go I would never have known the building existed. The club was run by two brothers by the name of Les and Ken Murphy. I brought the judo kit and was given a grading card. This was something totally different from anything else I had ever tried before. The club was called the Budokan and every Tuesday evening I would go hot footed up there and come back home aching. Learning to fall was the first thing that we were taught. I had a lot of practice! One of our teachers was Pat Roach, who was an all England Brown Belt champion, he later passed his Black Belt grade at the first attempt. I remember one throw called an ankle sweep where you had to attempt to pull your opponent off balance and sweep his ankle from underneath him. To do this to Pat Roach was a physical impossibility. I would have had more luck with a telegraph pole.

Although I had developed other interests I was still going out with the lads and having the odd half pint of shandy. I was a tall lad over six foot and looked older than my years, so I managed to slide into the snug and get a drink. If I chatted a girl up at a dance and found out she was older than me I would always add another couple of years to my age. This nearly led me to an early downfall.

One girl in particular was 21 and I only 16 but told her it was my 21st the following week and did she fancy going to a dance at Ansells Brewery. I met her on the Soho Road and we walked down through Lozells and into Aston and down to the brewery. When the dance had finished I walked her back into town to where she caught the bus outside Greys as she lived the other side of Brum. I arranged to see her again the following week, but things got a bit serious and she wanted me to meet her Mom and Dad. I stopped going dancing for a while and she eventually gave up.

I always said I would be my brother's age when I got married. I wasn't to realise that within three years I would be walking down the aisle at Bishop Latimers. My brother courted a girl who lived in Peel Street, just off the Green, her Dad and Mom kept the Sir Robert Peel, an Ind-Coope house and her name was Summerfield. She was born in Bromsgrove Street in the town, which probably made her more of a Brummie than us. They then went and lived out at Kings Norton, finally coming down to the Green to run the Peel in the late 1940's. My brother did his National Service, came out, got engaged and they married in 1957, that was what I wanted, but it wasn't to be I am glad to say now.

It all began at the Hippodrome. Working at the bakery they would treat the bread lads to a tea at to Co-Op rooms in the High Street and then to a show at the Hipp. You could imagine what it must have been like, possibly a hundred lads, out for a good time, taking over the one side of the circle. The show on that week was the Adam Faith Show with the John Barry Seven, and a comedian who didn't stand a chance with us lot. I was in the last row with the rest and behind us were three girls. They told us to shut up as we were a nuisance. Naturally we had to have our say, and one thing led to another and we got talking to them. We offered to meet them the following night outside the Gaumont in Windmill Lane, Smethwick. My girl told her friends "don't take it for granted and bring your purses just in case they don't turn up". We did and we started a long and happy life to come. Her name was Margaret Glasgow.

I took Margaret home to the obligatory tea, it must have been serious, as I had only done it once before. After tea we were clearing up and our Mom asked Margaret to take the scraps over to the miskin. A look of bewilderment came over her face, "what's a miskin?' she asked me quietly, "it's the dustbin" I replied, not understanding that only Brummies used the saying. "Well why don't you call it a dustbin?" I had no answer it was one of those words that was always used and I had been brought up with. I am glad I told her, otherwise she may have been walking around the back yard all night. Margaret lived on the Warley side of Smethwick which was only a couple of miles away, but sayings that we had, she had never heard of. She should have been proud, she was courting a Brummie and her life would now change!

Chapter 20
A New Direction Now

We went around as a threesome for a short time, but eventually split up, so now we were a couple. Margaret lived in a block of pre-war flats at the bottom of Thimblemill Road, they were classed as cottage on cottage. One big kitchen and a lounge, three bedrooms and a toilet and bathroom (which was inside the house), this meant no more traipsing up to Bacchus Road to the Public Baths. Margaret had a good Dad, he was down to earth and we became good friends in the years ahead. He worked at Earle and Bournes in Dudley Road opposite the hospital. He was a sheet metal roller. Margaret's Mom, Eadie, worked at Scribbans the cake makers off Windmill Lane, Smethwick. We had many ups and downs over the years but as time went on we did get to like each other.
Margaret worked at Woolworths on the Bearwood Road as a supervisor and me a mere bread boy. Even at this time I was still going to judo school which I eventually gave up for some serious courting and dancing with my mates, but slowly I was outgrowing this part of my life. Almost every week I would be at the Co-Op hairdressers in the town to have my hair done. George Badley who was a barber there, lived in Wellington Street by us, he used to come on his push bike on a Sunday morning to cut our Dad's and my hair when I was a lad. I worked at the Co-Op until I was about 18 then found a job at Scribban's Bakery in Goode Street at the top of the Flat. I was told later that when they pulled the building down it was like the Pied Piper of Hamelin when thousands of rats scrambled away from the ruins. I used to have a drink in the Hydraulic or the Abbey Vaults by the bakery then I would get the bus home to the Green, to have a quick wash and brush up and meet Margaret. I hadn't a car in those days, so it was either the bus or shanks' pony. Margaret and I went dancing every Monday at the Thimblemill Baths. I remember the Ronnie Hancock's Band and the lead singer Susan Maughan. Sometimes on a Saturday we would go into town to the Locarno or the the West End, but mostly it was the Plaza in Rookery Road. So here we are back on home territory, my mates would be there and it wasn't far from the No. 11 bus that would take us back to Smethwick. On Thursdays we would meet at the steps to the Art Gallery and go to the pictures. In those days there were no multi-screen cinemas, however, each cinema showed a different film and each had a different feel to them. Walking around Birmingham not so long ago, I only counted one and that was

the Odeon. No more were the Gaumont, the Futurist, the Forum, the Bristol and the Scala. They say you shouldn't look back but I do, and regret that the next generation have missed out on the variety that I once took for granted. Even most of the local cinemas have gone like the Winson Green, the Regal on the Main Road, the Grove in Dudley Road with wicker chairs on the first floor to the circle, the Gaumont in Windmill Lane, the Elite in Handsworth, the Palladium in Hockley Brook and many more all within striking distance. All you would need was the entertainment page from the Mail or the Despatch. Sorry to see them all go.

On my 18th birthday Margaret and I got engaged. We had a party, but it wasn't like you would hold a party today at a Pub or somewhere like that. It was in our front room, but it surprised me just how we managed to get so many people in our little terraced house. Like I said before, in those days people were born, christened and married all in the same area and I was no different. Margaret and I were married at Bishop Latimers on the 3rd August, 1963 and we lived over a shop on the Bearwood Road, Smethwick. Mark who is my eldest son was born 12 months later at St. Chad's on the Hagley Road, even though when he came out of hospital with his Mom back to Smethwick, he would have only been a couple of weeks old. He still classes himself as a Brummie. I'm proud of him.

Even then I would go back down the old end to have a drink in the Railway Inn with our Dad. You move away from a place but there seems to be that invisible elastic that keeps on pulling you back, but eventually we moved right out of the area to a place called Great Wyrley in Staffordshire. It seemed like the other end of the world but houses were cheaper and it was of course the 1960's and us kids wanted something different for out next generation, with green fields instead of terraced houses and back yards. Two more children came along, Tracy and Maxine. I still worked in Birmingham and would have moved back because of the travelling. We never did, but it was still a pleasure to go back to see our Mom and Dad down Eva Road and all the old memories would all come back, old friends would get married and they would move on. I suppose you could liken to it to a wheel all the spokes went to the hub, as like our parents did, we did the opposite and moved away.

I still go down the Green now, even have a walk up the entry to our old house and stand where the gas lamp was. I think about the hours we played round it. Hopscotch until we couldn't see the chalk marks. Losing marlies in the shadows of the gutter and waiting for that shout from the top of the entry from our Mom to come in and likewise other kids would have the same. I can shut my eyes and picture long summer days during the holidays when the street would be full of kids eager to play football up our entry until Mrs. Hardiman came out and told us off. Tieing two door knockers together and knocking on both doors, hearing the cursing from behind the respective door as they tried to open them.

These and many other memories come flooding back. Having my first bike and showing it off in the street. Marching down Foundry Road on Church Parade past our street when our Mom would stand with other proud mothers. Going out with a new suit for the first time. Bringing a girl home. All these things are precious to me and nobody can take them away. I can't see somehow that the next generation will be the same, but that will be for them to find out. Also they will never relish a bath in front of the fire and as we grew older it was th public baths in Bachus Road for 1/6 (7.5p), you would get soap and a towel, but we always took our own. It wasn't too bad in the summer, but in the winter it was murder to come out all warm and dry and to walk down home on a cold night. If that didn't keep you fit nothing did! So perhaps the next generation to follow our Mom and Dad's would make sure they would get it right.

This story has been a small stroll down a small part of Birmingham, not remarkable by any standards, but a reflection of a post-war lad who was told not to play in the horseroad, but 20 odd years later saw a man walk on the moon. I think we experienced the greatest of technological ages that man has ever seen and absorbed it. From a Midland Red bus ride to Stourport, a tram to the Lickeys or a train journey to the seaside for a holiday, we now take for granted a flight to a more sunnier clime.

It was while I was on holiday, in Tenerife of all places, when I thought about writing this book. I had thought about what Mr. Powell had told me many years ago and I decided that it was our turn to tell of Birmingham as we found it. We are the ones who have probably seen the biggest changes. Unfortunately apart from photographs of demolition and re-building of the city centre no one thought of taking photographs of such areas as ours (The Green).

I hope that I have brought a few memories back to those of my generation and if I have been successful them I am happy.

Chapter 21
The Railway Pub, Not Exactly a Village Inn!

It lies on the corner of Victoria Street and Wellington Street and at the last sighting, it was all boarded up and derelict with paint peeling off and looking in a sorry state, but that wasn't how I remember it. The building has two storeys, public bars at ground level and assembly room over, the private quarters above that. At the time of telling this story, Harry Moore was the licensee with his wife Margaret, but more about that later. The pub had typical half frozen windows with the name of Mitchells and Butlers etched into them, sloping sills that stopped kids from either sitting or kneeling on to look into the bar, and I suppose from adults from putting their pint glasses on. It was a hallowed place where grown ups seemed to go in with a straight face and come out all merry. I couldn't understand what all the fuss was about with this beer, which I used fetch for our Gran in a jug I once tasted it, I thought it was horrible and our Gran's ale was safe after that. We used to fetch it in large quart bottles and the barman would put a sticky label over the stopper to make sure that it wasn't tampered with. It didn't bother me as I have said I preferred a bottle of Tizer. Although, like a good many more, I acquired the taste later in life. As I have said Harry and Margaret were the managers. They had no children which was a pity as I thought he wasn't bad to us kids, if we were rowdy, playing outside the pub or playing up the Soap'ole he'd come and tell us off, but never in a nasty way. I chucked a snowball one winter when I was a kid, it was aimed for someone else but unfortunately hit him square on the back of the neck while he was walking down Foundry Road. He gave me a right rollicking and left it at that, but all my life he never let me forget it. Even though when I was a married man with children of my own, he would recite the story to others in front of me. They retired in the 1970's and went to live in Bromsgrove. Some years later I took Mom, Dad and Margaret my wife over there to see him and his wife. They lived in a brewery cottage behind the Brittania Inn on the main street, he was helping out at the pub at the time and do you know he still had to recite the story!

At about the age of 14 I joined the fishing club and would enter all the contests, this would now be the purple patch in my life as I felt now to be accepted in a mans world. On a contest day (which was always held on a Sunday) we would be outside the Railway at 7.00am awaiting the coach, slowly others would arrive with rod bags, baskets and nets, the odd one coughing from dragging on a fag. The coach would turn up, the back of it would be opened for the tackle, and be placed in there reverently so nothing would be broken. Then everybody would pile onto the coach, last but not least the beer, crates of it would be passed onto the coach, Albrights and Family Ales, and off we'd go, we wouldn't have got to the top of Foundry Road when our Uncle Bert Morris would announce who wants what? at that time of the morning. I could never understand how they could drink beer, our Dad used to buy a couple of bottles which he would save for the riverbank, they would go straight into his keepnet and into the river to keep cool. The men were great, I loved to be in their company, their chatter, their jokes apart from the occasional 'bleeding' or 'sodding' there was no real bad language, at least not to my face. They were all characters on their own. I still remember some of their names, there was Jackie Whit who lived up Winson Green Road, he was the secretary, and Bert Morris, treasurer who came from up Smethwick, there was Teddy Payne who was a butcher from out of Foundry Lane, his pal big Eric a green grocer from Booth Street, Handsworth, George Baker, 'Phippy', Tommy Jelly, Dave Dilloway, our Dad's mate from the Birmid, Johnnie Evans, a couple of relations Harry and Charlie Wood. Our kid used to come but he was a bit under the thumb as he'd just got married. Every summer there would be an annual match and all the families would go, husbands, wives and kids and would always end up at a pub on the way home. Tired and grubby. The coach would drop up back at the Railway (before closing time of course). Off home would go the mums and kids, and the dads would have a last swift half. It was a great club. I fished in the Christmas Fur and Feather when I was about 15 and won a half bottle of Drambuie, I never did get to taste it, I had to give it up.

When I was 18 Dad was proud to take me in there for my first drink. When we sat down to play dominoes, Harry Moore leaned across the bar and said to me "Did your Dad know that you've been slipping into the passage for the passed 6 months for a drink?" When I was 21 I booked the assembly rooms above the bar for a party for the grand sum of 10/6. By this time I was ready to move away from the Birmingham area, and I wanted to make sure that we all had a good time. As I said Harry and his wife retired, the pub would never be the same again and a succession of managers induced some of the regulars into building their own club, and about 300 yards down from the Railway Inn was built the Merryhill Social, before that a spokesperson and a committee were formed, led by Arthur Painting who lived in Perrot Street. He held the first meetings in his front room. I don't know of all the original members who started the club but our Dad was involved as was our Uncle Bob who drank round at the Foundry Tavern, Johnnie Holloway, Freddie Simpson, Jodder Jordan and a few more. That was finally the end of the Railway and I never went in there again. I look now on photos when Harry Moore and his wife had their last night there with a farewell celebration and see all the people that made one little part of

Birmingham such a part of me. The old dears sitting up one end of the bar, Aunts Sarah Anne and Ada Wood (from Little Eva Road) Mrs. Cutler and other ladies, at the bottom end were the men playing dominoes and crib like Freddie Castle and old 'Whitty' and others that I have mentioned. They were all part of this little story, without them the pub would have been featureless. Fortunately I was to witness all of these lovely people. Sadly most of them have left us now, but if I sit on my own and shut my eyes I can hear and see them on either a riverbank, a breakfast trip or just a good night down at the pub.

Farewell Railway Inn you may be all boarded up now with paint peeling away, but you will always be a happy memory to me.

Presentation night of Harry Moore and his wife at the Railway pub on their retirement. Dad is third from the left, next to him is Freddie Castle, Jodder Jordan, Freddie Simpson and Johnnie Holloway.

Dad Fishing.

Chapter 22
The Final Chapter

I must conclude this little walk down memory lane with leaving Winson Green. Margaret and myself went from Bishop Latimers on a wet afternoon in early August 1963 to our reception at the Thimblemill pub up Bearwood. We went up the Green, past the prison, round into Dudley Road and on into Smethwick. I was now married. Just short of 20 years of age, and still classed as a minor. I could be called up and fight for my country but was still not allowed to vote! And on top of that I had to have written permission off our Mom and Dad to get married. Anyway the reception went off well, and at the end of the night my pal Jeff brought us back down to our old house. We spent out first night in our Mom and Dad's bed. The next day we were up early as we were going on honeymoon to Jersey and had to get to Elmdon. That would be the last night that I would sleep in that little house.

We came back a week later and moved into a flat above a shop on the Bearwood Road. It was strange. A week or so previous it would have been our Mom that would be getting me up for work. Now it was our Margaret. It was a different feeling getting used to travelling to Scribbans bakery from another direction. On the first week I even went to catch the 96 bus to go back down the old end; habits die hard! That was the worst part of it, the long trudge up Weston Road to catch the B82 from outside Dudley Road Hospital.

Eventually a new life and new surroundings soon blurred the immediate past. As I have said before the invisible cord would always be there while the family still lived down the Green, but as time passed by, one by one the grandparents passed away. Our Aunts Mary and Alice, and Uncle Bob bought a new house up the Queslett Road. Mom and Dad moved out of Eva Road to live in a multi-storey at the bottom of Lozells Road. They were both very happy with central heating and an inside lavvie, new furniture and panoramic views. No more traipsing over the yard for them now. They put in for an old people's bungalow, and after a time they moved down Friary Road, Handsworth Wood. Practically to the spot where Mom used to clean all those years ago at the house of the Canning family. By this time all of the close family had either passed away or moved. Most of my old mates had got married and left the area, so there was practically no one left down the old end, only memories. I still had to go back though, just to make sure it was all still there. It was and still is.